Keisha-Louise Sparks is an accomplished young woman who has recently become a director of a charity. In her spare time, she writes poetry and reads a variety of books. But most of all, she spends time looking for inspiration for her poetry.

*I'd like to dedicate this poetry book to my darling mother,
Donna-Marie Sparks.*

Keisha-Louise Sparks

FEATHER LIGHT POETRY

AUSTIN MACAULEY PUBLISHERS™
LONDON • CAMBRIDGE • NEW YORK • SHARJAH

Copyright © Keisha-Louise Sparks (2019)

The right of Keisha-Louise Sparks to be identified as author of this work has been asserted by her in accordance with section 77 and 78 of the Copyright, Designs and Patents Act 1988.

All rights reserved. No part of this publication may be reproduced, stored in a retrieval system, or transmitted in any form or by any means, electronic, mechanical, photocopying, recording, or otherwise, without the prior permission of the publishers.

Any person who commits any unauthorised act in relation to this publication may be liable to criminal prosecution and civil claims for damages.

A CIP catalogue record for this title is available from the British Library.

ISBN 9781788232951 (Paperback)
ISBN 9781788232968 (Hardback)
ISBN 9781528953306 (ePub e-book)

www.austinmacauley.com

First Published (2019)
Austin Macauley Publishers Ltd
25 Canada Square
Canary Wharf
London
E14 5LQ

The completion of my dream could not have been possible without the loving support of my beloved friends and family. They have shown their love and support throughout this process, and I am so utterly grateful. Thank you.

Apologies to Myself

Dear hands, I'm sorry for making you reach out for my other half, when I know they will never appear.

Dear heart, I'm sorry for every time I've made you skip a beat, for a person who left me after I'd fallen.

Dear tummy, I'm sorry for all the unnecessary butterflies; I promise it won't happen again.

Dear mind, thank you for always protecting me, when I go after someone who doesn't love me back.

Dear legs and feet, thank you for carrying my body when it's broken, and thank you for always moving on when I struggle to do so.

Dear ears, thank you for never listening to the people who hurt me. And finally,

Dear mouth, thank you for biting my tongue when I want to say something I don't mean. And thank you for always smiling even when I'm sad and my heart is broken into a million pieces.

Mother

To watch you sleep peacefully on the sofa, is a blessing to me.
Although you'll never know that I care for you so deeply, that my heart aches.

I often find myself staring at you, wondering how someone so hard-working and beautiful

could ever have a daughter as useless as I.
Every time you sing or dance, I think there she goes again.

My miracle mother, full of love and grace, the reason for my entire being.

Little do you realise that you're the only reason I get out of bed at all.
The only reason that I am still alive and breathing now.

You are the only reason I smile, when all I want to do is curl up in a ball and cry.

So mother, my hero, my saviour… thank you.

I love you

Coffee

Coffee, oh what a beautiful creation.

It is the first liquid to touch my lips in the morning, my morning kiss and cuddle.

The reason I have enough energy to leave the house, or even to last the day.

It keeps me warm on the coldest of days, brings me happiness on my saddest days.

Encourages me when I'm unmotivated, gets me moving when I've no get up and go.

This is my favourite beverage along with water, of course, it's my liquid cocaine, the only drug that completes me.

It's a part of me; without it I can't live… It's my happy addiction.

The love of my life, so I've come to the conclusion that if my future partner cannot make good coffee, then all is lost.

The Theory of Missing You

When I wake up and you're not there, my heart stops, my chest tightens, and everything moves in slow motion as if the world is coming to a stop.

When I go to pour my morning coffee, all my blood drains from my body, when I suddenly realise that I no longer have to make two cups.

When I go to leave the house, and I say "see you later" and don't get a reply, I just want to break down and cry right on my door step.

When I'm in my local coffee shop; watching the world go by and you're not there to comment on how people are dressed or where you think they're going.

My coffee no longer tastes the same… it suddenly becomes a dull bitter drink.

And when I finally get home and climb into my bed at the end of a busy day, and I feel how cold the sheets are, that's when I realise just how much you meant to me.

Now you're gone, and there's no way for me to get you back.

Because, you walked into my life with so many words but left in silence.

How Do You Say Goodbye?

How do you say goodbye? To your childhood, I mean you're told to grow up, but nobody explains how.
Do you just sit down with the childish part of you and tell them to leave because it's time to be an adult?

How do you say goodbye? To your best friend when they're no longer in the same city as you, or they no longer talk to you like they used to because they simply don't have the time.

How do you say goodbye? To your favourite pair of shoes that no longer fit you. And you can't just throw them out because you have so many good memories of 'you' in them.

And last but not least...

How do you say goodbye? To yourself when you're no longer the happy, smiley person you used to be.
Because you're now a caffeine-addicted maniac, who has insomnia and only sleeps three hours minimum a day. Because there's just so much to do.

Can someone please just tell me! How to say goodbye!!

Will you remember me;

When I'm gone will you remember how I said, "I love you"... to you every day without fail?

Will you remember the way I'd laugh even when the joke wasn't that funny, just to humour you?

Will you remember how I'd dance and sing around the house, just because I couldn't keep still or quiet?

Will you remember how I take my coffee… or what my favourite colour is. Will you count all the stairs in the house, so you never lose track of the way
I'd run up and down them just to get my heart beating quickly?

Will you remember how I'd talk to myself, because the most interesting conversations a person can have is with themselves. I know you said I was insane because of that.

But dear love of mine…

Will you remember me?

Maybe…

Maybe if I hadn't said what I did, then you wouldn't be sitting staring into space.

Like I had just sucker-punched you in the face.

Maybe if I had been more honest from the start and told you, that I didn't feel the same.

I know what I've said has hurt you but…

Maybe if you hadn't cheated on me, told me it was my fault, and then proceeded to make me feel so worthless that I constantly felt as if I was walking on egg shells.

And maybe, just maybe, if we had noticed that our entire relationship was fake and wasn't real.

Maybe, if we had noticed that we were living like mechanical parts of a clock. And we were just counting down the time until everything came to an end.

Cold Blood
(A View of a Serial Killer)

Murder is wrong they say,
But all I hear is go kill and play.

With my first victim, I played hide and seek kill. It was quite easy it took just one bullet.
The second time I murdered someone,
There was a lot of blood; it was so much fun.

To hear the screams and cries from each victim, it fills me with such delight.
Each time I stab, strangle and break my victims,
I laugh at the blood that spurts out of them every time.

The blood is such a bright shade of red; you can tell it's FRESH.
It's hard to believe that with such little effort, I've killed someone dead.

If you asked my parents they'll say,
I didn't turn out exactly how they planned.
They'll probably blame it on my friends or the television,
but personally, I blame it on their lack of love and neglect.

Because that is what made their beloved child become a twisted, sadistic serial killer.
Who enjoys chasing people whilst singing, and dancing. And in the end, she kills them.

IN COLD BLOOD!

Things Kids Say to Their Mummy

Mummy, why does the moon only come up at night?
Is it because it argued with the sun? Or does it not like mornings?

Mummy, can I have toast and cereal? Why not?
Can I have chocolate then? Can I have sweeties then? Why not?

Mummy, I want that teddy! I promise to be extra good. Pretty please, Mummy, I really, really want that teddy.

Mummy, can I play in the living room... can I use my paint? I won't get it on the floor... Maybe.

Mummy, do I have to have a bath tonight? I don't smell... you do! I don't want to!

Mummy, can you read me a bed time story? *Little Red Riding Hood*, please.

Mummy, can I sleep with you tonight? Thank you, Mummy.
Mummy, I love you to the moon and back.

Anxiety

My heart is heavy, my eyes weighted shut. I know it's morning, and I have to move from my bed eventually.
But I just lie there, my chest feels tight; I can hardly breathe. The anxiety is crushing any hope I had, that the day would go well.
I can hear my mum shouting up the stairs, that it's morning and it's time to get up.

I just about manage to muster the energy to move out of the safety of my bedroom.
When I'm out I begin my routine to escape my house, and enter the hell called the 'outside world'.
Count to ten, take steady breaths, walk slowly to the door, open it... lose my footing, pretend I'm okay... have a mini heart attack when I come into contact with anyone else.
When I reach the bus-stop, I put my headphones on and lose myself into my own little world of music. Forget that I'm outside until I reach town.

Town is busy when I get there; I walk at a quick hasty speed to get to the coffee shop. I practically pass out once I'm sitting down.
I drink at a snail's pace, because I can't bear to leave the sanctuary of the coffee shop.
Once I'm brave enough I get the bus home, when I get to my stop I practically run off.

When I burst through the front door, I say I'm home... and head straight to my room where I sit on my bed.
I take slow steady breaths to calm the rib-breaking heartbeats, that have almost killed me during the day.
Later that night, I climb into bed, relief sets in and I finally drift off to sleep. Knowing that tomorrow will be another anxiety filled day.
But at least my bed is safe.

Unwritten

Only when I close my eyes, do I see everything I've never said or written. I have it in my head, how I thought or felt, but have never said or written it down.

I'm foreign to the feeling of importance, as half the things I wish to say are irrelevant to any conversation I've ever had.

So instead of looking stupid or like a moron, I never say or state how I feel; therefore, the other party is blissfully unaware.

Of what I actually want…

I ignore everything that my mind and heart come up with, because these two have plenty of time to be mischievous later on, when I'm on my own.

So, for now I will withdraw any emotion, and keep everything I think and feel locked away.

Which means it will never be said; thus, it will also stay unwritten?

Insomnia

Laying in darkness is my nightly routine, I try to sleep but my body will not let me.
I'm a prisoner to my own mind; it's too energised to sleep, and overthinking is what my mind does best.

Especially when there is nothing to think about! But no apparently there is like...
Did I lock the door? Do the animals have enough food? Did I record that television show? Have I turned everything off? Did I do everything I needed to do today? Did I set my alarm? And so on and so forth.

It's an endless list of useless things,
and I can never seem to get away from it.
When you've got insomnia sometimes the only way you can escape staying up until stupid o'clock in the morning...
is to make yourself physically and mentally tired.

So instead of counting sheep like every other normal person does,
I find myself curled up in a ball every night at 4 am like clockwork... crying. Because that's the only way I can fall asleep nowadays.

Trapped

Please accept my words of sorry. I'm always making mistakes.
I can't seem to tell my left from my right; it's like I'm lost in the world without sight.

Even when I'm not in the wrong, I still say "sorry". Maybe it's because that's how I'm wired.

I make sure everyone else is okay, before myself.
I think I'm broken, because if I wasn't, I'd stand up for myself.

But when I try the word can't seem to escape. It's like my mouth is stapled shut.

I've always known that my opinion is not necessary, nor valued by others.

I guess that's why I'm always so quiet, as it's best to keep my mouth shut instead of upsetting the people around me.
I am permanently trapped. And there is nothing I can do about it.

So instead of kicking up a fuss, I will repeat the process every day.
I will do everything they ask and want of me.

Because that is all I know.

Things You Should Know Before Dating Me

1. I don't like mornings. Or Mondays, at all, so the worst time to talk to me would be then.
2. I am addicted to coffee, pancakes, and strawberries and sleeping. If I haven't had any of these... I will be a horrible mess.
3. I talk to myself every day, because the best conversations I've ever had are with myself. Crazy, I know.
4. If you can't find me in your bed at 3 am... it's because I'm in the kitchen making food.
5. My family means everything to me. I will quite happily drop everything to help them. They will always be a part of my life.
6. I'm a major Disney film fanatic; you will get used to me singing and dancing along with the films. Don't worry I'm not insane, I just haven't grown-up completely and I doubt I ever will.
7. If you can't find your hoodie, it's because I'm either wearing it or have it at my house... and no, you won't get it back.
8. I will sometimes seem like I am somewhere else, but I'm daydreaming; it happens quite a lot. I hope you can get used to it.
9. I have crippling anxiety and depression that makes it hard for me to get out of bed sometimes. You may find me one day under the cover in a ball crying my eyes out. Don't worry; you've done nothing wrong. Just hug me, tell me everything's okay and that you're there... I promise I will stop crying eventually.
10. If the next day I act like the night before didn't happen, please for me, can you do the same.
11. I struggle to show emotions, so if I don't tell you I love you every day... please know that I do but just can't put it into words.

12. Finally, when I'm at my weakest all I want to do is run... please be the one to stop me. I will thank you for it later.

Ex

I still miss you; I spend most of my time wondering what you're doing.
We were together for so long; I'm still trying to get used to being alone.

I remember your birthday; every year I have to stop myself from sending you a card.

Sometimes when I'm asleep, I dream you're still here. But when I wake up, and you're not here, I practically break down into tears.

My days are filled with thoughts of you, and how I used to spend every waking moment with you.

I still feel your lips kissing mine. Your hand on my hip… the way you ran your fingers through my hair.

I can still hear you tell me you love me. Even now… after two years of being apart.

But now we're like strangers and it kills me. You were such a big part of my life; you were my salvation when I was down and upset. I can no longer come to you for cuddles when I just want to cry.

I miss you so much, my heart is broken but you have moved on and you are fine.

Dear Love

Dear Love, Can I just ask why?

Why?!...

Why do you always send these perfect partners to me, and then tear them out of my life?

Why do you give me butterflies, when you know it won't last?

Why do you mess with my head, so much I can no longer think straight? Why do I feel useless when you're not around? Why?!

Can you tell me? Can you? Because I'm at a complete loss!

I don't know what to do; my heart is crying because I have run out of love… I have run out of YOU!

So, LOVE, where are you?
Where have you gone?
Because I miss you!

Bipolar

I have manic episodes at least twice a day, I talk so much that I forget to breathe... until I'm told to take a breath. I have insomnia; it's linked to bipolar and I barely sleep two hours a night most days... but then there are days when all I do is sleep, because I can't bear to move from my bed.

Not just because of my crushing anxiety or depression, or the fact that if I leave the house, I'm scared that I'm being watched or that I'm going to pass out from the fact that I am even outside.

I get frightened by my own voice sometimes... I have loud noises I mean they really f**king terrify me. I have panic attacks when I'm being looked at. Everything around me is scary and unknown to me. Sometimes I have suicidal thoughts. I see myself cutting my wrists, but all that comes out of the ribbons is the brightest shade of red. *Hanging is a good idea* the voice in my head tells me so, because I wouldn't have to talk, or be scared of my surroundings, hate myself... or think of hurting myself on a daily basis because I would be dead. You can't think if you're dead!

I avoid people, even my family, and I put my headphones in and cannot hear or see them. It's wrong I know, but there's nothing I can do about it. I want to be closer to them but every time that I try to get close to one of them... my chest feels like it's being crushed, and I become unable to function correctly if I physically touch other people—even if it's a hug. I just stand like a statue thinking "What do I do? I'm scared, why're they hugging me? Do I hug them back? Do I say thank you? Do I push them off?" But instead I just stand there unable to voice what I'm feeling because my opinions don't matter; nobody else cares how I feel.

I'm always tired, even if I've managed to sleep the night before. I don't enjoy anything that I used to anymore, instead I am an empty shell of what I used to be. I'm always crying and I don't know why... it's like my body is falling apart from the inside out. I need help but I'm too scared to ask for it, let alone the fact that I try to ask... my voice fails me, my lungs deflate and I am unable to breathe.

By every partner I've ever had, I've been called a 'Psycho' maybe they're right... I mean one moment I'm happy and smiling, then the next I'm standing upright screaming and crying uncontrollably unable to think, unable to stop anything that I am doing. I find it difficult to tell anyone but my mum that I love them. I'm scared that that they're going to walk away after I've said it. I've already been left so many time.

I talk to myself every day, even in front of people because if I don't do it I feel completely alone, even if I am completely surrounded by people. The voices in my head are family to me, sometimes they say the most horrible things, like. "Why don't you kill yourself? It'll be easy no one will miss you but us," but sometimes they say the nicest things like, "you're not alone you have us. You are amazing, you've got this and if you're scared talk to us. You can't sleep tell us why, and if you don't know let's go for a walk."

It's stupid, right? The voices in my head are there for me whenever I need them, but they're also what's killing me inside. I feel like if I don't talk to them it'll only get worse... I'm taking medication, but it doesn't work. I've told the doctor but he just tells me to give it more time. He also suggests that whilst I wait for it to start working, that I go outside and try not to stay inside too much as that doesn't help.

I just remember sitting there nodding my head in agreement thinking that's easier said than done. I go home feeling down trodden and defeated. I'm completely unable to think, talk or breathe... so I just go to bed.

But before I go to sleep, I lay on my back looking at my ceiling, and I whisper "I have bipolar, I'm scared and alone... but I survived another day. So that must count for something, right?" I say goodnight to the voices in my head, close my eyes... and drift into the blackness of my dreams.

Dear Death

Why do you take away everyone I love and care about?
How can you just steal away the people who mean everything to me?

Do you get joy out of breaking my heart into a million little pieces?

I mean is it that fun to watch me break down and cry?

Do you have a list of things I love so you can take them away? Are you starting at the bottom and working your way up?

Could I just ask why?
Or could I ask if you could stop, not forever just for a moment…

I would offer to meet you and talk, but you're an imaginary person I've thought of…
Obviously, you, Death are real, but for me to think you're a person is stupid. But Death… you've hurt me more than anyone else can. You know my weaknesses; you know what make me tick.

So, I know this may seem harsh but, Death, I hate you… but I also love you. Because without you, the world wouldn't work the way it's supposed to. So, Death, I hate you but thank you.

Princesses

Princesses, when you stand in front of me with your arms stretched out, looking at me like I am your whole world, my heart jumps out of my chest, and I can see it skip a beat just for you!

I spend all my time with you when I babysit. I enjoy our cuddle and film sessions… our talks of who loves who more. You always insist that you love me more.

But, princesses, I have loved you since the day your parents told me I was going to be an auntie. I thought, "How could my life get anymore prefect, I have two beautiful nieces now. I would give my entire life to you both just so I could see you both smile, because your smiles are the light of my cloudy days." When you were babies, I remember holding you, thinking I am so blessed to have you in my life.

Obviously, your parents will do a great job of looking after you, but let me tell you that no matter what happens my door is always open for you. You can tell me anything; I will keep your secrets. I will make sure that no matter what time it is, in the day or night, my phone is on. So even if it's just to call to tell me you love me, I will answer. And when your parents are bugging you about your room, I will defend you because I will always be on your side no matter if you're in the wrong or right.

Because, princesses, that is what an auntie is… an auntie will look after her nieces no matter what, will become a shoulder to rely on when you're too scared or upset to talk to your parents. An auntie will always have ice-cream and films because who doesn't love ice-cream and films? …An auntie will always have a spare bed for you to sleep in, and if not, she will always give you her bed instead.

I love you both so much, you two are my two little princesses, my favourite girls. I am so privileged to have nieces like you.

You

When I first met you, I thought you were arrogant, weird and annoying.
Every time I was with you and our friends, you'd joke around telling them you were going to kiss me.
Not because you liked me, but because you wanted me to pay attention to everyone else instead of my books and music.
You said I was an expert introvert who did not belong in such a loud-mouthed group.

I will never forget the day I shocked you so much your mouth was agape, and you were shaking.
All I did was defend our female friend. I shouted and stood upright in front of a man twice my size and told him to f**k off!
He laughed until I hit him for calling me a whore; everyone, even you, stood frozen. Not knowing whether I had snapped.

After the man left, I just sat down and carried on reading as if nothing had happened. But you would not leave me alone.
Telling me you wanted to look at my hand, after you repeat the same annoying sentence seven time, I reluctantly held my hand up so you could have a look.
But instead, you kissed it and made me speechless… So, in return for that, I kissed you full on the mouth, filled it with enough emotion to make even Cupid blush.

Everyone gasped in shock even you after I'd finished… I smiled and told you, "You taste like vanilla ice-cream," and you looked confused for a moment…
I let what I had said sink in… you looked into my eyes and said,
"And you taste like heaven." Thinking how cheesy that line was, we both began laughing like children, who had just been caught eating cookies.

And in that moment between a kiss and a laugh… my world was perfect.

Dear Grandad

When you died a piece of me died with you...

You were the perfect man, wrapped up in toffee candy. My magical granddad, who no matter what I did always cuddled me tight.
You were my mum's knight in shining armour, my warrior ready to fight without any notice.
I remember when I was just a little girl in your garden crying, and you rushed out, picked me up and started to sing to me. Your voice soothed away the pain better than any kiss could... although your magical kisses were an added bonus.

My mum loved you so much that I swear her heart could burst out, toffee flavoured love... When you used to call and talk to her, she used to smile the biggest smile. It was a smile that I'd only see when she spoke or saw you, her daddy wrapped in toffee-flavoured candy. That was your favourite candy apart from fudge; you always had some in stock at your house.
I'd always stand in front of you and ask, "Grandad, can I have one of your candies?" and you'd always take a moment to think about it... then say, "Only one poppet, only one."
I'd savour that one candy for at least thirty minutes, all the while you'd cuddle me and ask if it was nice... I'd always nod and say, "Yes, Grandad."
It's hard to believe that you, my wonderful, loving granddad wrapped in toffee-flavoured candy, could ever go to sleep and leave me behind... You left me on my 10th birthday, but now every year I remember you.
I sing and dance to songs that remind me of you; I still cry now— even though it's been ten years since you passed.

But Grandad, I loved you with a love stronger than love. I don't eat fudge anymore... but I always have a toffee or two in my bag...

Just for you!

A Letter to My Sister and Brother Who Are in Heaven

Even though I was born after you both, I feel like I have known you for all my life.
My sister and brother who didn't survive long enough for me to meet. But is it weird that I feel you with me even though you're not here?
I mean I feel you tell me not to do something, when all I want to do is do it.

When I was alone and feeling so depressed that I considered killing myself… is it weird that when there was a blade to my wrist, I felt your hands on my wrist stopping me?
Is it weird that when I'm crying alone I feel you cuddle me and tell me it's all going to be okay.

I know this sounds completely insane, but I do believe that you're both with me… helping me, advising me just like you would've if you were alive.
I'm sorry that I never got to meet you.

But I guess that's just how life works, isn't it? But you're both my angels in the sky… and my bright stars at night.
And my goodness how bright you shine, I mean you two are the first stars I see along with our nan and granddad… I hope they're taking care of you.

What does heaven look like? Are there a lot of kind-hearted people? Is good taking good care of my big sister and brother? Will I be able to find you when I die?

Dad

When I was little, my first love was you, Dad. I think every little girl's first love is their dad... or their brother.

But mine was you, my tall dark-haired father... with brown eyes that could see into my soul if I let you.

When you took me to see your parents (Nan and Grandad), I remember being in their garden, chasing their ginger cat...

But I could never catch him, I'd always fall... you'd come running out scoop me up into your arms, and cuddle me tight saying "Pickle, you're okay."

You'd always catch me if I fell and if you didn't. You'd make me hot chocolate as a "Sorry, I wasn't there" kind of gesture.

Looking back now I think now how much things have changed, all for the better now that I'm an adult and an older sister at that.

To think that I'd be an older sister to anyone shocks me... but I am and they are wonderful bundles of joy that if I could.
I would wrap them up in cotton wool... just so they wouldn't injure their little hands.

And I, who looks at them with love and adoration, only see the face of my father... my first love reflected back at me.

So, I think it's safe to say that Dad... I love you and no man could ever compare to how much I love you.

Sister

Boxes packed, ready to leave…

I know this is what you need, you've lived in a box for far too long. You need some room to breathe.
Beautiful house to make yours, to create precious memories with that little girl of yours.
Working hard to make it pretty and homely, to welcome us as guests through your door.

I've grown to watch you rebuild your entire life more than once. Each time I've watched you glue each little part of you back together.
A role model, a girl could grow to be, your little girl is following you without thinking a beat.
I see everything of you in her, how strong she will be… she will be able to stand against the hardest winds and seas… all whilst counting 1…2…3…

Every day you will see, how good a mother you have been. As every day you wake up and count 1…2…3… just like our mother did, you see.
A little girl grown into such a level-headed woman with a little girl of her own, how life gives these wonderful gifts I do not know.
But big sister of mine, let me tell you this… No matter where you or your daughter roam.
I will always be there in the shadows to lend you a helping hand, a cuddle and a chat. Because I will always be your sister, and you will always be my best friend of which no can replace.

Can I Just Ask...

Can I just ask you to stop? Can I?
I mean every word you say, is suffocating me. Like you're trying kill me. Every syllable is like a bullet wound to my chest, and I am the target to your word games.

Can I ask you to never speak again?
That may sound like an impossible task; I know how much you love the sound of your own voice.
But let me tell you, that your voice still gives me that feeling of annoyance, and I hate that.

Can I ask you to never look at another human being?
Because I don't want you poisoning them like you did me; I still feel the poison you left behind flowing through my bloodstream.
Like a parasite sucking the life out of me, purely for your own enjoyment.

Can I ask you to never breathe again?
No, I didn't think so, but it was a good try, I suppose.
I wish you would stop breathing though, because you are just a waste of oxygen... you pollute everything and everyone around you.

I know, I know what I'm saying is horrible, and I would apologise but... I... can't, I just can't.
So, to whoever reads this... be careful what you wish for... because what you wish for may not be what you actually need.

Madness

If I could I would time travel to a different time, just to see what life was like then. Were the people as ignorant as we are now?

If I could, I would change everything in the world to make it peaceful, but that would be foolish. Because it wouldn't make anything right, as people will always find a reason to fight.

If I could I would fly in the sky like a bird, it would be nice to see the world how they see it. Does the world look different from that height? Will it look more peaceful? I guess that I will never know.

If I could walk on water, I'd walk to the middle of the sea and look on in shock and awe, at how the landscapes have changed.

If I could talk to God… I'd ask him/her what the purpose of humans are, and why are we the way we are? I'd also ask for a hug because who wouldn't want to hug God, right?

And if I could, I'd look into the faces of the people who bullied me and forgive them for what they did. I'd offer them a hand and tell them they are always welcome in my home.

But I know this is all just madness, and like a candle in the dark it will extinguish.

Dream Guy

I am tied to you, by an invisible red string.

Although I've never actually met you. Which may seem and sound strange?

But I've seen you, in my dreams... and I know you see me too, because you talk to me.

I know you're real even though other people think I'm weird.

Every time I'm in town, I swear I see you out of the corner of my eye. My perfect dream guy, who I only ever see in my sleep.

In my dreams, we sit on a beach at night and look at the stars.

We talk for hours whilst drinking wine, you pull me in tight cuddle and kiss me... And as the sun rises you look into my eyes and I look into yours.

I see my reflection and that's when I realise, you have helped me start loving myself again, and I know this may sound vain and weird. But I would like to say thank you... for helping me find myself again.

I hope one day that I finally get to meet you, hold you, kiss you and tell you that dream guy... I love you!!!

A & E

Overworked nurses and doctors walk at a quick pace, no time to stop and rest... they've got a job to do.

Annoyed patients who have sat in the waiting room for more than four hours, seem to think it's the nurse's or the doctor's fault. They don't take into account that the people they abuse have already been on shift for more than eight hours.

Dealing with patient after patient must be hard; you can tell they're suffering from tiredness. Dark bags under their eyes, but too busy to stop and take a breath.

They spend their day repeating the same questions... "On the scale of 1 to 10 how bad is the pain? Have you taken any medication to help with the pain? Where do you hurt specifically? Can you put any weight on the area in question? Does it hurt?" and so on and so forth.

Half-an-hour breaks are all most nurses or doctors get; that's barely enough time to think, or eat... once their break is over, it's back to the long list of impatient patients who also seem to think they know better that the people who are treating them.

No matter what day it is, there will always be a drunk, or a person who is high and it's the job of the medical staff to help them... but how can you help someone when they don't want to be helped.

I'm sure at some point the staff must want to just stop in their tracks... find a vacant area and cry, sleep... or just take a moment to breathe, have a cup of coffee or tea... then go back to their chair and begin their routine once again...

And I know that it's a job that they love or enjoy... but these people don't get enough credit for what they do.

A&E is a place that you sit, wait and get seen to as quickly as they can get to you. Patience is needed. But once they've helped and you're going home… remember to say "thank you". They really will appreciate your words.

Christmas Cuddles

Eyes pop open like a champagne bottle bursting, sparkling wine…
Overflowing energy and excitement fills the entire house, songs and games are played.
Kids wait patiently for their parents to give them their gifts, cheerfully opening each one with glee.

The occasional kiss is shared between partners, husbands and wives cuddle whilst listening to their children or family laugh and play.
Mum's in the kitchen cooking her roast dinner, and making sure everything is ready for Boxing Day… little treats are given to the children to eat.

Late evening meal, everyone has a cracker to pull… tell me a joke, Dad!! You'll hear the kids say… and he'll always reply…
"Why did the chicken cross the road?" "I don't know, how?"
"To get to the other side!"
You all laugh to humour him, but enjoy the company that Christmas brings… as it's the only day families spend together fully.

Night draws near… P.J's are on and movies play on the television… everyone comfortable sitting in silence as the snowman walks in the air.
Kisses goodnight… and wishes of sleep tight… Finally, the adults can settle. Cuddles on the sofa, glasses of wine or bottles of beer. Kisses under the mistletoe… and, phew, Christmas is over cheer.

New Year

Welcome to the New Year... it's the year your life comes to a crashing halt. You're completely unaware of this, of course.

But here's how it starts, you'll go on a diet because of this 'New year... New me' crap.
You'll get a new haircut, or buy new clothes or things for yourself because you believe it'll help you in this new year of opportunities.

I don't think you realise how deep and far you're going to fall, work gradually starts to pile up, family and friends demand your attention. However, there are not enough hours in the day to delegate for every task at hand.

Time slips through your hands like water rushing down a stream... you can't seem to catch your breath.
So instead you quicken your pace, you seem to think that everything will be easier if it's done faster.

Then a sudden realisation sweeps over you like a surprise ran fall in summer... you begin to slow down, spreading what needs to be done between your days.
You have lists beyond lists for each day, but as you go you tick every single thing off. Soon you're done with everything and it's only September... time to buy for Christmas... and get ready for the next New Year to come.

Hacks for Your Period

1) Be prepared to curl up in a ball, with a hot water bottle at hiss at the male species... because during this time you will hate them with a passion.
2) Always have a hidden chocolate/candy/sugar stash because you're going to need sustenance, that will make you feel better... but just a pre-warning you will hate yourself afterwards and think you're fat. Which will lead to you crying.
3) Have a box/pack of tissues everywhere you go... because you will be a nervous wreck and could burst into tears at any point.
4) Make sure you have some super romantic movies that'll pull on your heart strings... and of course will help you believe in True Love again.
5) Ice cream will be your best friend... along with chocolate, and you favourite pair of P.Js.
6) Have an emergency pair of panties in your bag, just in case you overflow because it happens!
7) Always carry these things in your bag;

- Tampons or sanitary pads, whichever you may use.
- Wet wipes
- Paracetamol/ ibuprofen
- Spare pants
- Chocolate

It may be embarrassing but you'll thank yourself for being prepared for your busy day ahead.

8) Remember that you will not die from this... unfortunately you'll have to deal with this for a few years.
9) Mother Nature does not hate you; she's just as bummed as you are at the fact she has to bleed for 5-8 days straight. So please don't blame her.
10) Do NOT punch the misogynistic male who says the following things:

- A period can't be that painful.
- Being kicked in the balls hurts way more, I guarantee it.
- Man-up (What the hell does this even mean! I'm a woman!)

And so on and so forth but they're just men, so of course they wouldn't understand. But just look at them and wish that their first child is a girl… because they will come to understand it, one day.

11) You will need your friends so invite your girls over and have a couple glasses of wine and a bitching session; you'll feel so much better afterwards.

12) Once you're at the end of your cycle, you'll feel much better and more energised so go outside and take the world by storm, buy that dress you want, don't forget the shoes either, you deserve them.

Count to Ten

I see your face go red... like you're a bomb about to burst.
You've got so much anger built up inside of you; I'm surprised you haven't lost it before.
You're always pleasing other people before thinking of yourself. Is this what being a mother/father is about?

From time to time your voice shakes, your eyes twitch... I can see you slowly coming undone. So, of course, I have to push you further... it's my job as your daughter.
But instead of shouting and getting annoyed, you close your eyes and count to ten. You then send me to my room until you're ready to talk to me again.

Your patience isn't like that with anyone else but your children... I saw you shout at each other once... but I think it's safe to say that Mum won that argument; she shut you down quickly with the comment of "It's my bloody house so I'll do what I bloody well want, you understand!" I loved that. Mum stood so tall and made you feel so small.

The next day, everything was back to normal, so I started to misbehave... But this time all you both did was count to ten... grab me and hug me. Not knowing what to do... I hugged you back and told you I loved you.
Getting ready for school, I witnessed you both kiss and say, "I love you, and see you later." It was the sweetest thing I've ever seen.
If this is what counting to ten does... then with my children I'll do the same.

Smile

I know it's hard; I can see you breaking apart from the inside out. But, darling, please smile, because I know it hurts but it will all get better.
I know its cliché for me to say that, but it has to get worse for it to get better.

I'm always here for you through any rainy day you have, I'll be your light in the dark… your shoulder to cry on, your personal cuddle pillow when you need warmth and love.

I will never judge you, I will be your wall of protection, and you will never be without me… you will always have me… and little do you realise that I've loved you for many years now… it kills me inside to see you so down and upset.

You're so conflicted between your family, friends and your partner. Every time you're with me I see you completely relax, like a weight has been lifted off of your shoulders.
We sit, cuddle, watch television… and talk for hours… and as we sit there I see you smile and it is a completely relaxed happy smile.

Is it bad to say that in that moment, I fall for you all over again. I have to hold myself from kissing you because your smile is so breathtaking.
You're more yourself when you smile… and because you smile, I find myself smiling along with you.

So, please, just for me can you smile?

Fairytale

Every little girl wants a fairytale to happen to them, to find their perfect guy or girl, to live happily ever after.
But is that really the definition of a fairytale? What about being happy on your own, even if you have a couple of dozen cats... Can't you just be a warrior of a women standing tall like a tower?

Fairytales are when you find yourself; you look straight in the mirror and see a queen standing before you. Your crown may have slipped a little, but damn you look fantastic... you're my own version of brilliance.

Every time I see you acting strong and proud, I want to applaud you... you need your own standing ovation, everything you say sounds like a symphony. Even your words sound like a song, you don't need music to make your own melody.

Your fairytale is made up of memories... you've made so many; isn't it hard to keep track? You tell me no, and explain that with each memory you create, you gain a new friend or experience. I notice when you tell me this, you have the biggest smile on your face... I can tell that you're truly happy.

Your fairytale has four children in it, and each one you love equally. You have so much love to give, so much information to share. I insist that you should write some of these down... but you say I always remember my own set of rules, and so will you.
I don't get what you mean, but I'm sure I will once I have my own version of a fairytale with my own little princesses and princes to pass my wisdom to.

Please

Please don't take me for a fool, I may be clumsy sometimes but I am no fool.

Please don't think that I can't live without you, because I can... I mean how do you think I survived before your arrival? I worked really hard to be who I am now.

Please don't tell me you love me, when you clearly don't. I can see that you don't; I'm not stupid. I can see that you don't feel the same way.

Please don't tell me I'm wrong or that I'm stupid for believing in what I believe in, you have beliefs just like I do... and mine are not wrong, dull or stupid—they're my reason for living, the reason for my bright smile.

Please don't push me aside, I am just as important as you are. So please try to understand why I stand so tall... and why I will always be there for you.

And finally, please believe me when I say that I care for you very deeply, and I would put everything on the line for you. Will give you all my attention, like a mother does for her baby. Like a sister does for her brother, a husband for his wife.

You will have my undivided attention, you will have my everything. So even if you can't give me everything, please at least give me something.

Puzzle Piece

You and I go together like cookies and cream... we're two of the same, cut from the same cloth.

But why does it feel like something is missing...

Lately all you do is talk about how much regret you're got. And what you wish you would've done when you were younger.

My love I see your life light, draining from your eyes. Like a candle being blown out by a sudden gust of wind.

Over time I see how much you've aged, the way your once youthful skin has begun to wither and wrinkle.

You still knit, sing and bake... you've got so much energy in you still... and you always manage to surprise me.

But you always wait for me, so you can do your puzzles... it's like I'm the missing puzzle piece that you've spent your whole life looking for...
So, my love, if I'm you're missing piece, you must be mine.

Cry

Huddled in the corner like a terrified kitten, is going to get you nowhere.
But you know this, yet you still sit there like a child who's just been scolded, by their parents.

The only time you ever move from that spot when you're this upset is when I stand in the doorframe with my arms open wide.
Like I'm inviting you to stay the night in my grasp; you've always felt safe with me.

No matter where I am, you always seem to find me—your safe haven, your personal protector—for this is role you've given me.
You're a grown man, yet in my company you act like you're a child again.

We play games every day like it's normal; it's a ritual you have to do or else you feel physically sick.
This is what high functioning anxiety is for you, a compulsive disorder that you have control over.

When you were young, you got severely bullied for this... you contemplated suicide until I stopped you. I slapped you hard across the face then proceeded to cuddle you whilst you cried.

That I made a promise to you, that no matter where or when you needed me I'd be there. I'd protect you from anything that scared you, that made you feel inferior, or like you weren't important.

But when you sit in the corner of the room, huddled in a ball crying like a toddler who has lost their favourite toy.
I can't but look at you and want to cry too; I have anxiety just like you but I hide every single bit of it.

Because I wouldn't want you to see me so weak, when you're already breaking. So, my adult-like toddler, let's play a game, let's colour in, lets cuddle and watch films all day until your heartbeat slows enough for you to stop crying.

Time

Sitting in the middle of a grass field, makes me feel completely at ease.
More at ease than when I was with you; somehow the smell and feel of freshly cut grass makes me relaxed and calm.

I've spent most of my life running... after you.
I think maybe it's time I stop. You clearly don't care for me like you say you do.

Time is like my best friend lately; it seems to slip by without my noticing it. It's helping me get over you.
I even forget what day it is sometimes, because I'm too distracted by other things.

Trying to move on is hard, but I think it'll be easier once you're no longer around... once you're out of my air space, once you're miles away. Maybe once that happens, I'll be happy.

But I suppose for now that's just a wish that'll never come true, because you come running to me like a child who needs his mummy... whenever you're down, upset or in trouble.

But it's in these moments that I'm thankful to Time, because with every day that you come running back... time moves quickly until you're gone... and then moves slow until you come back.
So, thank you, Time, for being my guardian in everything.

My Demons

I can't escape my nightmare; they follow me everywhere...
It's like I'm a child unable to sleep because of the monsters under my bed... and they're called Depression and Anxiety.
They're like little gremlins, causing trouble everywhere and leaving a mess in their wake.

If only I could shut them up and tie them down, so they couldn't go anywhere and ruin anything.
I've lost so much because of them, I don't think I could stand to lose anymore.

Unfortunately, they have other plans, They always wait until I'm at my happiest... That's when they pounce on me like a lion who hasn't eaten. They suck up any energy that I have, and once they're done they leave me completely broken and tired.

This happens to me every time I ever feel happy or positive about myself. I've tried my hardest to cope with them both, but it gets so hard sometimes...

I've started doing activities to get my mind off them, but it's like they've taken human form.
I see them everywhere I go, like they're trying to get my attention...

In the end, I go home... and sit in complete darkness like a psychopath waiting for its prey... and the prey is them. They will not win! I will conquer my demons; they will obey me... even if it kills me. I will beat them.

Innocent

Your eyes are so bright that they could practically blind me if I looked too long. They still have that childlike shine in them; I'm glad that it's still there... because that means you haven't been corrupted by the poison around you.

You still have that childlike smile and laugh; it's really quite infectious...
It makes me feel at ease knowing that you still have your innocent ways that means no one has harmed you or made you feel less than human.
You always look at me like I'm your whole world... that's when I realise that I'm looking at a reflection of myself.

I see you in there... it's okay you don't have to hide... I can see you. You're my inner child who will never grow up and that's okay... I know you're scared and you've been hurt by so many people, but you've also been protected.

You're not alone, and you never have been, so please don't hide.
Tell me all the secrets you've kept, let your adult self-help you... we are one of the same... we are the same person, it's just you were unable to voice what you felt or went through.

I know you can't explain what you've seen... how you felt when it happened.
I know you hide everything deep within, but you don't have to hide from me anymore.
We are the same person after all, so please come back to me. I will protect you. We can survive this together.

Because we are innocent.

You're Too Young

You're too young to be so sad; what reason have you got to be sad?! Too young to be depressed, too young to be suicidal, too young to hate yourself... You're too young to know what love is, too young to know what you want. These are just some of the things people say to one another.
Just thinking of it scares me—this world is so cynical that we put people down from the moment they're born.

You're too young... too young... young. What does that even mean?!

I wasn't too young for you to lay your hands on. I wasn't too young when you were bullying me and tearing me apart.
I wasn't too young when anorexia, depression and anxiety got a hold of me and made me feel so damn worthless. Where were you when I needed you?

If I'm too young then why does it feel like the whole world is against me? Why does it feel like I'm sinking in quicksand, and the only way to escape is to sign my soul away.
You say I'm too young for love, but do you even know what love is... because I don't, but that's not going to stop me from trying to find it.

You're too young to be able to do that...
You're too young to travel that far on your own; it's not safe.
You're too young to know what's right or wrong for you.
You're too young... too young... young.

Yes, I'm young, but weren't you also young at one stage?
Or are you exempt from this... is it your way or the highway?

You're too young to be this reckless.

You're too young to feel so empty… too young for anti-depressants. You don't even need them.
You're too young to be depressed… trust me, it's just a phase it'll pass. You're too young… too young… young.

I know you think I'm too young… I know you worry about me and you believe I'm too young, but I've already seen too much, been through too much.

To be told that I'm too young.

Wish

Every day I wish for life to be a little easier, a silly little wish I know but I do it every day.
I have a little list of wishes that I carry in my pocket, just a list of silly little wishes. But I still carry them… I carry them like a weight around wherever I go.

It's not heavy, and it doesn't bother me… but I know it's there.
If something was to happen to me and I were to die… Refer to wish three because that's what I want to happen once I'm gone.

If I was to go missing refer to wish three and seven because they're both connected in some weird way.
Every wish has a reason… and there're instructions for them too. I know it's strange, but it's just a thing I have… in a way it's my own personal comfort blanket that no one else can see unless something bad was to happen to me.

But if I was to tell you my biggest and most important wish.

It would be that I wish to be happy… I mean isn't that what everyone wants? To be happy I mean…

Scars

I know you see them... I know you want to ask me how I got them... I see you stop yourself. I see how you look then choose to ignore it because you don't want to jump too deep into my bloody stained skin. Especially since you haven't got a boat to sail in the red sea the flows out from my veins.

Everybody has them... scars... some are visible, some aren't, but that doesn't mean they aren't the same! Yet you still believe that just because you can't see them, they aren't there... just how offensive can you be.

I see you stare. I see how you look at me with pity... I see it, you can't hide it. It's the same look someone gives an animal when it's injured... I'm not an injured animal... I'm a human being! And I've survived this long.

I know you judge me for them; I know you do... because it's easy for someone to judge when they don't understand, and I wish you would let me help you understand... because then maybe you wouldn't look at me like I'm crazy or I'm unstable. I'm not... trust me, I'm not.

Sometimes I wish I could just erase my scars... because then you wouldn't look at me, like I'm damaged, like I'm broken, like I'm not good enough.
But I know that I am... I know that I'm good enough. I know that I have survived and these scars are just war wounds... they're memories from my past that I cannot change... they're one of the reasons I keep moving forward.

These scars do not define me... I know who I am without you telling me.
My scars are mine!

Why?

Why?!

Why do you just stand there? Why don't you move? Can't you see what's going on... won't you help me?

I'm dying from the inside out; my body is killing me... it's rejecting me!
Why can't you see it? Does it have to be a physical wound that you can see before you help me? Does it?

Why won't you believe me, when I tell you that I'm not well? Why don't you help me? I need you... but you're not helping me!
Aren't I supposed to be important to you? I guess family mean nothing, when you've gotten everything you need already.

Fine! I'll save myself... but let me just ask you this.

Why are you so damn selfish? Why did you leave me behind?
Why did you lie to me about everything? Are you too scared to be truthful for once?

I guess that I'll never know the answers to my questions... because no matter how many I ask you.

You will never tell me why!

Hurt

Everything you say to me, cuts me like a knife. You never think before you speak.
How stupid can you be?
You still think you're better than me!

I have always been in your shadow, always done as I was told.
I've had enough now, I'm getting my life together. And walking out the now, wide-open door.

Even though I have left you behind.
You still manage to crawl underneath my skin... You're like a rash that won't quit.
Everything you do hurts me.

I can see that it does not bother you, that I am on the floor, gasping for air.
My whole world falls apart, when you're near. Why can't you leave me alone?

Must you contact me?
Must you come back into my life, when I've only just managed to get over you! You don't think about the consequences of your actions.
Because in the end all you're doing is hurting me... but you don't care.

Fallen

Sleepy eyes look back at me, as the sun rises over the trees. You stayed over for the night, the first time in your life…
We fell asleep cuddling and talking to each other.

I wish that last night could last forever;
I don't want this perfect moment to end.
But we must get up, we must go back to our normal daily lives.

But would it be bad, if I told you that I had fallen for you! In the worst kind of way, I mean I love you…
Everything about you is a gift to me.

I love your bad habits, your past and your future. You're everything I want… everything I need.
My heart aches when you're not near, it's like it is slowly breaking apart.

Can you rescue me?
Will you kiss it all better and make the pain in my chest go away?
I've fallen for you, I want to know everything about you.
I want to know all your dirty little secrets, all the lies you've ever told. What's your mother like? Do you have any siblings? Your favourite colour… your worst nightmares… your fears…tell me all of them. And I will tell you mine.

Because I have fallen for you! But I think you know that. Because you have fallen for me, too.

Gone

Sitting in a deserted church, is like admitting you've committed sins... but know you cannot change them, no matter how hard you try.

You pray for some help... some clarity from your day-to-day life. Yet life isn't that bad... I mean you're still living, right?

Your chest is an empty cavern; there's a hole where your heart should be. Your hands still twitch from the feeling of being slapped away...

You're a lost child searching for you mother... but you can never find her.

Maybe you were already gone by the time I found you.
You're like a tattered blanket that no one needed, you're broken, you're torn...

Nobody wanted you before me... to you I'm the light in the dark. You don't see that you're just fine without me.

Every day I tell you that I like you, I tell you to breathe, I tell you everything I love about you... I leave little notes to brighten up your day.

Notes that say... your eyes are like a starry night, they're forever shining. Your hands are strong, and can bind anything together.

Your heart is a light that helps me see in the dark... Your smile can make anyone want to smile with you.

Even though I do this for you every day... I still get the feeling that you're not actually here... that you're actually just going through the motions...

You're a robot; all you know is ones and zeros... you can't see between the lines.

Maybe it's my job to help you with that...

But there's only so much I can do before...

I gradually fade away...

Become something less than myself...

And eventually I'll be gone, too.

Just like you!

Wake Up

Walking like a robot without a heart,
I sit and watch you… intrigued to know what you're going to do next.

You've lost so much already,
How have you not completely lost your mind? Or have you already lost the will to live?
Are you just going through the motions?

Some people say that, what doesn't kill you only makes you stronger… Is that really true? Do you feel stronger?
I don't think you do… you're just staring off into space like you miss your home planet.
Are you even human anymore? Do you even have a heart?

If I stopped you from doing what you do every day… will you malfunction? Will you cry… like a child? Will you be completely at a loss?
For goodness sake… stop being so emotionless…

You're not alone… if you need help, ask!
I'm here… I'm just arm's reach away, reach for me.
Wake up!

Depression

I'm losing the will to live...
Losing the will to breathe, I spend my days walking like a zombie.

Believe me, when I say it's hard for me to even move.
I'm so hungry, tired... but these are feelings that I'm slowly becoming numb to.

I'm a disease and I'm eating you alive, nobody can see me, nobody can hear me. To them you look pale, you look ill. To them you need help, in the form of pills.

How does it feel to have an invisible illness, how does it feel to be alone? Come on let's go and see the doctor, let's listen to their medical opinion.

Don't you feel sick, I bet you do. I have that effect on people.

Ask for help... they'll say there's nothing wrong with you.
They'll put you down, they'll just say you're doing it for attention again.

Nobody can understand the invisible illness that you have, that's sucking your life out of you like a parasite.

But don't worry, I will never leave you. I'll always be nibbling your ear like a lover in heat.

Just ask me to help and I will.

I'll help you fall asleep; it may be painful, but you'll be safe and sound once it's done.

I'm the reason you're in pain.

So, it feels kind of ironic that I'm the one that can end you're suffering.

You listen and believe everything I tell you.
Would it shock you if I told you, that I do this because I love you?

Someone has to love you, right, and it's true I do love you. Why do you think I won't leave you alone?

Even the drugs won't get rid of me… but don't you love me too?
Isn't that why you stopped taking the magic pills, that they prescribed you?

I'm your own personal devil on your shoulder, I'm your depression.

But in a sick little way, you love me, don't you? Just like I love you.

Introducing the Writer

Hello, my name is Keisha and all the poems in this short poetry book are all personal battles that I have gone through and am still going through on a daily basis.

Throughout my life I have struggled with the way I am, but I have always had a passion for poetry and writing. When I first started writing poetry, I was scared that the poems I wrote were bad… and unskilled. I didn't realise that I had any talent until I shared some with my friends and they suggested that I send them to publishers.

Writing to publishers asking them to make my dream come true was the most terrifying thing I have ever done. There will probably be more terrifying things that will happen to me, but at the moment, it's the only one that has caused me to have a panic attack.

But when I finally received a response, I couldn't believe it! I started crying and set to work on completing this book.

Sorry that I've given you my little life story, but I will end it on this note… when you strive to climb over the hill of things stopping you from getting what you want in life, and once you reach the top, you will notice that there is a world filled with opportunities that one can only dream of. You've just got to chase after your dreams and grab them with both hands, because if you don't, you'll always be wondering *what if…* and that's a sucky way to live if you ask me.

Don't live your life in black and white… make it as colourful as you can.

Come into my world, take a seat, and make yourself comfortable.

Printed in the USA
CPSIA information can be obtained
at www.ICGtesting.com
LVHW051247151023
761011LV00016B/299